poems, a nickel apiece

jack babcock

To WRAP (Write Around Portland) and Ken Ballard (instructor) for help with my writing.

To Gloria Giddens for being a friend during some tough times.

And to Folk Time for all of the above.

Poems

Poems

Poems

Poems

Poems

Poems

poems, a nickel apiece

a pennyeach is too cheap recession or no.
pennies will go by the wayside and nickels too
in the meantime I proffer up a poem or two.

enough

am I a poet?

or am i just another guy
with a drawer full of poems

Yes, but one of them is
a Beryl, a Gem.

Author Notes: a beryl is a gem

erratum

who of us
doesn't make errors
is a poem
an attempt to
correct them
or is it also
erratum?

poetry by charles bukowski

it takes a lot of
desperation
dissatisfaction
and disillusion
to write
a few good poems
it's not for everybody
either to write it
or even to read it.

xmas wish

yes
olden days
getting the tree with gramps
at his farm.
and mother in Ireland:
they get an orange
in their stocking
and a stuffed animal
maybe a doll

and now they're gone
gramps, mom
and I live in the city
and eat tuna on a bagel
I quit drinking
but I am not able
to find life so sweet
as in the past
but if I try
life can be kind and simple
as in the past.

granddad

Gramps had a good mind. He drove to work
when he was 80. Did grain inspecting.

He harvested strawberries too.
He was quiet. Maybe he was not
intelligent. I think he was tho.
Based on the fact that his offspring
were.

Mostly I remember his kindness.
He was always good to people
no matter who.

What I think is odd is my
illness schizophrenia.
I could never have explained
it to Gramps. Dad yes. But not
Gramps.

He was all about fishing
berry-picking baseball
an old chevy truck strawberry
plantings and old barn.
my god gramps. help.

Gramps was going down

Cornell road in his truck
in the winter. Hit the ice
crashed and died. I mourn.

catnap

splayed out on the sidewalk
the calico cat does some
stretching some relaxing
whose cat?
I have only a guess.
house A or house B.

Mollie and I see him
on our walk
would I like a cat?
no not even if it is Herman.
for I can't abide a cat's habits.

besides I talk to myself already
better not to talk to a cat.

so that leaves a dog or a hamster
for pets.
and a dog is impractical
bathing constant walking.

so that leaves a hamster
named Dante.

bb

my bare butt
will I be published
my bare butt
am I a loser?
my bare butt
is life about noses?
No
my bare butt

america

(to the tune of god bless America)

Bog Blouse Ambeerikay
gland that I glove
gland beside her
glide by her
to the gland
that I glove
far a stove

from the mountain bars
to the corn dogs
to the facial
fight with foam
Bog Blouse Ambeerikay
my foam tweet foam

from the topless bars
to the pickles
to the lotion
light from Rome
Bog Blouse Ambeerikay
my foam tweet foam
Bog Blouse Ambeerikay
my foam tweet foam

path

It was so good to talk to you val
calms me down
I, a disturbed spirit
but you have some magic
some call love
good for my soul.
thank you val
from an admirer.

a lost poem

I wrote you
a poem
I can't find.
What good am I
losing poems
about you.
Oh! I should lose
poems about the president,
about lovers and such.
But Val,
you are so careful,
and I am sloppy careless.
But I've written a poem now.
This must be it,
I'll try not to lose it,
Val, sweet Val.

happy birthday

Laura's birthday is Tuesday
Val's is Wednesday
martedi
mercoledi
in Italian
ciao baby
I wish you well
birthday greetings
from your pal.

birthday

To a sweet grandmother on her birthday
    whose birthday?
    on whose birthday?
    why Val of course.

    love, jack

val

I made a bookmark
for you
but you want a poems
I'll have to write
it out
put it on a bookmark
Oh Val
I've never done that
I'm a little excited
a little crazy
what would you
like your bookmark
to say
For now it is
just a pretty picture.

for val

i promised a poem
not a heavy tome
will cheer us up or it will be
the death of me of us

oh val you are sweet
but I am not neat
the poem is for you
alas I am still blue.

the weather is nice
and that will suffice
this poem it is through
i still like you

next year

a dozen
purple roses
from trader joes
val
gave them to me

and all i
can give in return
is some
peonies
mrs. brooks
gave me the bulbs
years ago.
she passed
and now
i remember her
every year

and now val
gives me roses.
they will not
come up
next year.

a friend

I have a friend
who is on the mend

her smiling face
her accent
Suffice

now isn't that nice

Val I hope you feel better
and live a long life
that would float my boat

this is all I wrote

love, jack

poems

you want to
read my poems Val
that is well
a poem for you
takes a time
like good things
time
to get an idea
time
to say it right
getting it so you like it
getting it just right

oh Val, help
I can't compete
with your kindness
you are a rare person

in a way
I write a poem
for you every day.

brain

Val
I'm a little cracked
cracked out
I hear voices
all is not well
Life is often
a meaningless hell

but you talk to me
you assuage my pain
thanks
from a damaged brain.

on seeing mary oliver

I like my Oliver plain
like mom's pie dough
like my brain
But she was exquisite
read beautifully
inspired me
for she said
when she's finished
with a poem
she isn't proud
she is grateful
now I know
that feeling too

disappointment

Have you ever considered fella
that Emily is a lousy poet
and
that Shakespeare is a poor dramatist

Ha! I thought so!
You haven't!

Author Notes: just a thought

friends

Emily and I
    were homebodies
pot a tea
scoot the cat out of the chair
and stare
      at infinity.

Sylvia and I
were suicidal souls
I could see my body
crumpled bloody
broken
upside down
just socks
just socks

Sylvia and I were
    suicidal souls.

Author Notes: Emily is Dickinson. Sylvia is Plath

down the road

when we read Dickinson
it's awesome

yet

how glad we are
that Ginsberg
came along

so we could be
our self.

Author Notes I like both poets but I'm kind of scruffy for
Emily.

madness

Loneliness is my name
for that who's to blame
I mimic Emily
I write poetry
I seek out Sylvia
I look for answers and a mate
but I may be the mad Ophelia.

Author Notes: Emily is Dickinson. Sylvia is Plath. Ophelia is
from 'Hamlet'.

reading gertrude

Is Emily a good poet
and Sylvia too
or are they both rather poor
and why am i asking this question

they get put in books
a thousand thousand looks
they must be quality
surely not frivolity

well they are famous poets
and dont i know it
but Stein said there is no answer
and Stein is well a poet too
and I believe this
yes I do.

Author Notes: Emily is Dickinson. Sylvia is Plath. and Stein is
Gertrude Stein a modern poet

call it a poem

someone gave me a poem

it wasn't t.s. eliot's
book about cats
it wasn't joyce
it wasn't tennyson
or dylan thomas
or william carlos williams
they all would have received
an appropriately warm reception--------

no it was modern stuff
culled from the newspaper
I say modern i don't know really
what I know is
it was a drawing
and a photograph
and the artist called them poems.

well this is a liberal definition I mused
but it was not deeply original
It was art tho.
a drawing of a dancer
a photograph of lions made in stone.

it occurred to me that they were
unskilled at poetry
why I got no lines

but it raises questions
what is a poem really
a couple rhymes
a few lines
a glass of wine
finis.

call a drawing or a photo
a drawing a photo
are they poems?

lying lines

when the moon comes over the mountain
reading Richard Wilbur
      Sylvia plath
  middle night
oh god
don't I have a more tortured life than she
I hear voices
I should drink tea
read, write poetry

drink tea
read, write poetry
what if the end is near
drink til you're blear
plath's despair
is an enigma
I like
fig newtons, cheese, and beer.

bare naked

I'm reading difficult poetry
and looking often at pornography

sways in the balance

question

is Richard Wilbur
a good poet
is Sylvia Plath

they wear an odd kind of armor
keeping us from the truth

i can always look
at naked women
that gets old

poetry doesn't

It is fresh and new
even if literally
a hundred years old.

the lucky lady

how did it happen. I was going thru
my poems and saw one called pastrami ——
and I knew what this was — a reaction
to frank ohara's lunch poems —
what can i say. He wrote about his
lunch and what was going on with him.
Thus he wrote about a cheeseburger but
also art, but one work was called —
the day the lady died —
so I'm reading Frank o'hara
he's pretty good methinks
the lunch poems are maybe his best.
he writes about art and meaning
difficult topics.

umbilical cord

this was the unkindest cut of all
unless you count circumcision
I've had both
I've never performed either

but an umbilical cord

must have some important meaning
nourishment from ones mother
no breast milk —

but more to the point
I'm trying to decide if
I like Richard Wilbur peoms

I like two for sure
the one about a toad
and the one about Sylvia plath
(death of a toad) (cottage street)

but is that enough to call him a good poet
I think it probably is

the rest of em we can use
for wrapping paper?

dickinson

Seaside
how I miss it
I knew the town
like the back of my hand.
kinda.
I knew the thrift stores, the golf course,
the tavern, the hospital,
restaurants, fishing holes,
the candy store, rite-aid,
and especially the promenade.
It stretched a mile or two
in front of the ocean.
and by houses, a great many
of all kinds, sorta beachlike tho.

I would walk it early in the morn.
and late in the day as well.
It helps to have a dog with you.
Meet more people. see more things maybe.

And I would write keeping a journal
but often creative pieces, poetry etc.

poetry
I'm taking a class in modern
poetry on-line.

The instructor particularly
likes walt whitman, william
carlos williams, and bruce springsteen.
I don't particularly. Williams is okay.
whitman reminds me of stepping
in dog-dew, and springsteen god help us —

but we are also reading Dickinson whom I
            love.
she is electric. fascinating.

how many poems did she write.
Much mystery surrounds her.
like the question of how many poems —
and her poems are subject to
wildly divergent criticism.

poet at work

what's a good poem
keep it simple stupid!
everybody likes the Raven
one can conjure up this bird
the neighbor has a
crop of sunflowers
am I an ordinary suicide
and not a poet
Sexton Plath
don't blow it
So who is a good poet
as far as I can tell
people agree on Emily
but not Sylvia
wouldn't you know it?
I like simple stupid poems
why don't they
say what they mean
occurs to me
and Friend,
Emily we agree is Fine
what of Sylvia though
is she Repine?

blue iris

solitary blue Iris
looks like a cat
about to lap up some milk
dances a little in the breeze
makes quite a show
lonely thou
a cat ready for a nap
Blue Iris.

gold iris

a little patch
golden Iris
yellow they say
majestic though
lots of colors
yellow they say
elegant though
a little patch
golden Iris.

proud city

Proud city
I stand before you
your million tiny lights
are diamond stars to my eyes
I know you
for I know the earth beneath you
and the Sea that feeds you
and the Sky above you
these are all a part of me
and not not of you
Proud City
I stand before you
I know you.

b.s. in literature

sometimes i think
poetry is just bullshit
a desire to be with God
and this is impossible
and those sickening sweet rhymes
La naus.

But I gather up and go on.
and read recite write listen
to poetry.
For what else do I know.

concert

Beautiful as you are

A beryl in a drawer full of shells

I didn't like the music

But I had a wonderful time.

Author Notes: a beryl is a gem.

economics

its a terrifying time to be alive
the obvious things the violence
subtle things too
pleasure and all that goes with it
the economic system

valentine's day

I think of valentine's day
  as a week that is a dream
  we open our book and read:
  The season of Love
    begins our Valentine Days
  A week spent in simple ways
    light as a fairy
      on gossamer wings
        We fly
  Monday
    we sit and sew and
      make our cards
    For Valentine
      the ones near and dear to us
  Tuesday
    we prepare
      some light refreshment
    Some tea and cake
      for Valentine
        Dear to us
  Wednesday
    we Sing and Dance
      done with our cake
    we walk thru the Glade
      and whisper to Valentine
  Thursday
    we write our Poems
      our lines our Sonnets
    For those near and dear
      For Valentine
  Friday

we give our cards
sewn and sweet and secret
To friend, Valentine
Now we close our Book
for these were our
Valentine Days

Author Notes: a holiday I like

burgun

I like wine but I don't drink it
I like booze but I leave it alone
I like suds but I avoid them
water is just fine friend for now
I think of burgun tho.
I really think of it
am I really a drunk
I think of burgun,

Author Notes: burgun is yes burgundy. a drunks way of saying
it

color

I put on my scarf
for the cool day.
And I wondered
should I wear
the brightly colored one
or the drab brown
and I thought of nature.
the male often has the
brightest color.
so
you guessed it.
I opted for the colorful scarf.

feather

I find white ones, Gulls?
black ones, Crows.
But yesterday
I found a psychedelic feather.
A trip. A beautiful
iridescent Flicker feather.

Author Notes: feathers are usually pretty.

finch

The finches
at the window
brown necks
a little scarlet
seem hungry
eating seed
to watch them
is relaxing

Finch with
a scarlet neck
Finches feeding
on seed.
yes.

for L.

I had a finch
at my feeder today love
would I could hear you sing
tweet tweet is nice
but would I could hear you sing
you sing so sweet.

Author Notes: she has a nice voice

game

I love poetry
exploring the meanings
of things, of life

Charone likes sports
has favorite teams
follows them closely

I spose she gleans
some meaning from things

a bouncing ball
means what
that shes in the game
of life.

Author Notes: My caregiver digs sports.

college

my dad
wanted me to be an engineer
well I was good at math
but if I'd gone to OSU PSU
and studied that

I might not have met
three characters
three writers

Joyce Hardy Shakespeare

I met these gentlemen
at the U of O.

Author Notes: an english major

drink, drink, drink

the rain lately is stupid
it comes in buckets
it plods and plops
and I?

I wait and watch
and drink
oh how I drink

thinking there is a festival
somewhere
fiesta
c'est la vie

Author Notes: I don't know what to do, so....

love

At the beach
I walk down the strand
and stopped
and wrote in the sand:
L-O-V-E
but when I'd made the 'V'
I looked back and saw
how the wind had blown
the 'L' away.

Author's Notes: so it goes

eyes

the lengthening
                    shadows of the afternoon
this morn
your face
                dark sorrow around the eyes

your eyes
                shadow and sorrow
ah me
life!

imaginings

its a rare time - 5 a.m
a rare place   - a blank paper
a rare poem   - thus

I think I hear voices
can you know such a thing?

kill or be killed
duress stress
lie cheat and steal
can you know such a thing?

work

I don't want to work
what do I want then
fun gets old too

I want money to not be a problem
that means work does it not
make money writing
how does that work

who will give money
to read my shabby poems
and that's all I write really.

so I stumble along write poetry
Its what I do.

brittle

I break off twigs in winter
are these poems
I dig clumps of earth in spring
are these poems
well I know
by summer
a handful of dust
is a poem.

on valentines

its a pleasant day.
nothing has gone astray.

well one thing maybe.
I'm mentally ill.

a voice says as much.
who am I to argue?

But I do argue
Its just so damn mysterious

what was I going to say
happy valentines day!

paint

I wish I could paint
       I'd paint the seabirds at the cove
       the gulls the surfers
       the little hopping birds
       plovers

       I'm a terrible painter
       I know that
       Dave has an art teacher
       who says everyone can paint
       I cannot paint

       I love words tho
       I love birds
       I love the sea air
       the cove
       the gulls
       plovers
       the hopping ones

       I think I can write
       I can't paint tho
       the sea birds, the cove
       wind to your face
       an old coat
       hat scarf

       I love the seabirds the cove

       I can't paint but
       I can write I think.

Author Notes: the cove, Seaside Oregon

krugman

my brother
gave my other brother
a book of thomas friedman
columnist

plebian ordinary
it occurs to me

then there's krugman
I don't know he's right
but what a pleasure to read
one feels like
you're among the stars
this is rarefied air
or rare air anyway

so many hate him
say's he's a Marxist
I have no idea really
the columns make sense tho
and are sublime
in their writing.

calculus

is difficult
its subtle
I had trouble with it
oh I put in the numbers
crunched them and got the right answers

b's and a's for grades
but I knew not of what I did

algebra trig and less so geometry are easy to
         learn
but calculus asks these deep questions
is there a god?
what is life
what does it mean

I   was nonplussed
I crunched the numbers
and that was all--------

Author Notes: math puzzles me

california dreamin'

By the roadside
are California poppies.
Everywhere we stop
there is this orange flower.
I'm thinking of the past
meshed together with the present.
It's banal to see the
flowers
every half hour,
but
worse
is my mind
in a vise
being squeezed
of memory and meaning.
We go down
the highway.
My sixth time,
how is this different?
Well I'm not with
my parents.
There is no LSD either
this is a Volkswagen bus
before my breakdown
or is it
there is no half
empty fifth of booze.
We're straight cowboys
going down the road
looking at
California poppies.

shakespeare

I keep
Desdemona's handkerchief
draped over a lamp
and this morning
I peed on the floor.
Nearby is a teapot full of tea
strewn about were
last night's
daisies and peonies.
No daffodils though
I drowned.
I, the mad Ophelia.

augury

A voice last night
said 'shower.'
I need one,
perhaps badly,
but we defy augury.
After all
a voice said
to kill mom.
She's dead
and a voice has said
kill myself.

tea time

Often I think of tea
 Lipton's
Tetleys British blend
constant comment
now isn't that a way
to spend the day

Drink tea
forget
the lotus-eaters
the tea drinkers or is it
imbibers

I could spike
my tea I guess
or spice it

I relax with tea
read a book
and yes study
Calculus, Thomas Hardy
math and english
it helps

its healthy too
flavonoids
my taste buds

take tea and see
my eyes seem better
open

Teas
Leaves

rose petals
star anise
jasmine pearl
lavender
rooibus
chamomile
orange peel
pink peppercorn
safflower
darjeeling
sarsaparilla root
osmanthus

tea for me
tea I see.

when do you feel great?

not just great but really great?

I feel great when I finish a project.
last nite e.g. i wrote an essay for
modern poetry class. I was so
                exhilarated
when I finished.

I feel great at odd times too.
Yesterday on the bus going thru
the lloyd center mall. It was just
so lively and well beautiful.

Then there was a couple times
when I did use a substance to
feel great.

with tracy at the student art exhibit
at the college art museum under the
influence of mescaline

with Mark in his little gray volkswagen
out in the hills around Bethany. stoned
on pot. time slowed down.

roses

Leafing literally
through the pages of a playboy mag
But I find
on the pages an ad
Roses
Hybrid Tea
Grandiflora
Shrub Rose
Floribunda
It's Rose Festival
in Portland
Beautiful Women
and Roses.

scoring

down the blacktop
they go
the kids with their
toy hockey sticks
this is Oregon not Canada
the dad shouts out
'Michael score score'
Will the boys be
hockey stars some day
or casualties
4000 dead in Iraq
says the headline
I'm lame
I can't join in the game
a little lame goalie
who whispers
'score Michael score'.

Memorial

I took a walk
with my caretaker
I'm 60
it's memorial day
we speak of
vets and graves
flags and flowers
my brother and father
were vets
Uncle Adam
was in Okinawa
I tell
my caregiver
it was all a mistake
the lottery.

Park

Roses	at the park	fresh rain
Rain	walk the dog	poetry
Utrillo	Eliot	meaning
Umbrella	thru tedious streets	city bus

the library

spent many an hour
at the u of o library

read shakespeare
at the douglass listening room

and one day i'm studying
for a final exam
in modern drama
i'm reading o'neill

i'm depressed
i'm always depressed
so i thought nothing of it
but it lingered depression
and i finally thought
maybe i'm sick

so i toddled off to the infirmary
and sure enuf i had Mono

well finals were a breeze
since i wasn't there.
it took me weeks to really recover
what an odd subtle disease.

much tougher
was later in life
when i was diagnosed with schizophrenia.

like a voice has said
its a helluva tough illness
ah me.

can i recover i wonder
my hopes get up sometimes
only to be dashed

But i enjoy life
i dont have to work at a pissy job
i can write read paint play chess
make a mess
and try to recover
yes.

mescaline

you found a hustle......

in a tab of mescaline
in college
procured it for a couple friends
it scares me to think of those days now
like i told the crisis worker last night
i'm a straight cowboy
hell i can't afford to buy drugs
even if i wanted them
essentially i'm trying to put all that in the past
and live in the present.

but i recall one day some mescaline with tracy.
we went to the art museum and looked at
an exhibit of student art. i may as well
have been looking at utrillo, corot, van gogh and
picasso.

it was that good
and one nite i came home under the influence of beer
and peed against the wall
and made modern art.
i was that funky drunk artist Pizza sauce oh

well whats the diff
i ask whats the diff
between beer and mescaline.
beer is legit
mescaline makes you hallucinate

i know how the shrink wants me to end this
i'm better off without both
hell i have no idea really.

jasper

was an elephant
he tried to help his fellow elephants
he didn't want them to live in zoos
or be otherwise mistreated

he told them how in ancient rome
elephants were slaughtered
in front of crowds of people sometimes

that was the history of elephants
and today
was it that much better
surely but they were still
mistreated.

for example at Seattle's woodland park zoo Chai's
daughter Hansa only lived till six because
of negligence. then there was Bamboo and Watoto
Jasper thought they had been abused too.
and Sri had been forced to carry a dead fetus for 4
years.

Jasper was appalled. wherefore art there zoos he
pondered.

and what was he to do about it.
there were petitions and public outcrys

but the abuse continued.

people took delight in zoos and circuses
Jasper understood that but why the abuse
people didn't take care of the animals.
perhaps because it cut into profits.

Jasper himself was well cared for.
his trainer read doestoevski after all.
mistreating animals was just wrong.

doestoevski wrote that animals have the
beginnings of innocence and untroubled joy.
don't torment them.

And yet jasper knew it went on all the time.
not just elephants but all kinds of animals.
Jasper was a little more concerned
about the elephants. since he was one.

leaf

a scuttling leaf
a bird, a fly
break up the day
a rock found
in the street
kicked all the way home. 20 times.
i know what to do
and sometimes
i know why.

oregon

I quit the gonian. That is
the *Oregonian*. The daily paper.
It's a good rag I feel. But it is
not for me in some ways.

I don't read much of it. I don't
like them not taking a stand on
some issues.

I'm disappointed in some sections.
The poetry column for example.
Sour grapes? They rejected my poems.
No, I really don't like the column.

I will miss the comics, especially
Mutts.
But it's available on line.
And the crossword. Tho that is sometimes
an ordeal.

Then there are the ton of tragic tales.
I can do without that frankly.
When I quit the management at the paper
offered me a special rate. 2 bucks a week.
That's a good deal.
But i'm tired of going thru the ads
Sunday morning.

So I quit the paper! Yay!
Now if they don't strongarm me
into taking it all will be well.
I'm not joking. The Oregon mafia
wants me to take the paper whether
I want it or not.
Pee on them!

the 'f' word

I've never written
about a Fuchsia.
I never saw one
up close til today.

It looks like
me in surgery,
bottles of blood
hanging out everywhere
little pendants,
a deathbed.

The morning splayed out
against
the operating table.

Odd birds
taking a sip
at a lake.

The 'F' word
Fuchsia.

I've never seen
one up close
til today.

musica

en lo concierto
musica esta maravillosa
escuchar un poco
capturar por su belleza.

the rose festival

Love and Peace
Melody Parfumee'
Secret
Gemini
Watercolors
Kashmir
Pink Promise
High Voltage
Crimson Boquet

i feel a poem coming on

I've been lamenting
that the muse has died
I don't drink anymore
which is good
but somehow I lack inspiration

But I was thinking
of my loneliness
And felt a poem coming on
About 'H'
no, it could be tho
About 'GG'
I love 'GG'
Rather I want to
love someone so much
that I love the idea
that I love her
Anyone would love her
Surely I love her?

my life

the voices are still here they're
all around you

That was the answer I got when I said
to myself aloud 'my name is Jack
I live in Portland Oregon and I do not
hear voices'

yes that's at the core of my life
history an illness schizophrenia.

Shopenhauer wrote 'life is a
meaningless tragedy ending in
inevitable death.

And the past was wretched often
But I am happy now.

the concert

as beautiful as you are
a beryl in a drawer full of shells
I didn't like the music
but I had a wonderful time.

gull's song

Gulls
at the beach
Sea Gulls
Sea Swans
blustery day
Gulls at the Cove
Song of the Gulls
yes
far calls
yes.

sunday nite alienation

Saturdays are terrifying
in suburbia
in the afternoon the moon looms
but Sunday nite on a nice day
is aliention per se
The sun still glimmers
beyond the stars
this is despair, man
and at nite
an old TV show
goes on and on
they rerun it 50 times
on these Sunday nites
the same damn murder
in black and white
The sun is with us
day and nite.

grass

I got stoned.
Am I stuck
with these damn chess pieces
and foliage
vegetable matter?
Chess is a difficult game,
but if you play it in the
garden it's really inane.

taffy

It's snacktime,
and I hallucinate.
Why shouldn't I hallucinate
if it's snacktime

and I see
a little sack of
salt water taffy.
Peppermint,
oh, do let us be happy.

It's snacktime
and I hallucinate
peppermint
salt water taffy.
A little sack of

oh, do let us be happy.

gravel

Norm didn't get a funeral
nor did Charley I guess,
but inside the doors were
speakers with gravelly voices.
Norm calls me up and says
Milton Friedman is on TV.
I said, "Oh the walking talking baby."
Norm got upset.
Why do you call him that?
He writes great stuff on economics.
And I pondered Norm and his conservative
politicos.
I tell him those people
are not your friends. Norm,
I am.
I actually love you,
those people on TV
don't give a damn.
They're apologists
for free market capitalism.
They just don't give a damn, Norm.
But he persists in believing
the walking talking baby. Milton Friedman
was a genius to Norm.
So who was Norm?
He played the ponies
and drank a lot.
His love for free markets
didn't extend
to his personal prosperity.

the ocean on tape

close your eyes
listen to the surf

far calls
Gulls
seaswans

remember me
they shriek and say

Gulls
far calls

walk down the shore
impossible not to hear it
the ocean

the Gulls call.

dear old dad

if my uncle
had been my father
it's not like
I'd get up in
the morning
and do basic training
military stuff
but I would be
fukin women sure enuff.

there wouldn't be
a question like
am i gay or not
that would be
prohibited
my uncle tho
bless his soul
fought in the war
and I salute him.
glad he wasn't
my father tho.

crow's song

The bastard crows
Caw
crow's nest
caw caw
Ha Ha

Van Gogh
field for crows
caw caw
Angelus
Mithridiates
Cornfield
death
caw caw.

seagulls

i put up a blank canvas
and drew a seagull on it
and 3 more

i've painted and drawn gulls before
its a subject that works for me.

why is that
well i love the beach
and i love gulls

they represent freedom in a way
and beauty and nature and elegance and truth

i will paint my gull!

jay song

scree
scream
cacophony
voices
like what?

go to prison
kill someone
suicide
the Jay speaks his mind
cacaphony
of voices

noses
lie, cheat, and steal
why do some
find this real

Cacaphony of voices
a Jay song

noses
prison
you're a hitman
I'm a real criminal
voices
noses
Cacaphony
Jay song.

dresser

I wake and rise
I look at my dresser
it's small
Shall I compare H.
to my dresser
I rise and greet her not
she was small
subtle tight and nifty
like my dresser
I compare a woman
to wood
this little dresser
does her justice
shapes turned on a lathe
Fred does woodwork
a clock, a chessboard,
a picture frame
a letter opener.
I write poems
And I look at my dresser.

iris

It always scares me
that ferocious animal head
she has snapdragons too
while I instead
keep a few 'nots'
blue. a little field of
'forget-me-not'.

Author Notes: Iris its what I get

two irises

Two are open today
tomorrow three
and along the way
we shall see
on someone's special day
Iris will blossom
Hooray!

remember

I've been with
writers in the basement
for 10 years
10 years in the cellar
but a lot of good times too.
we've put out about 10 books
during that time.
it would be wrong to say
that I'm a much better writer
but some better surely
more confident.

my illness is schizophrenia
I write about it often
tell my secrets.
in 10 years
mental illness has become
a more talked about problem
and for that
we are grateful.

ice cream

the ice cream truck rolls by
with its insipid music
that sounds okay
if you're in a cheerful mood
but can be harsh
if you're drunk
and stumble outside
with your middle finger raised
while lady Brett gets off
I feel old

h

You came out of the blue
What a surprise
to see you
How difficult it was tho
to touch you
How easy it should be
How difficult truly

sunday afternoon

Cade is knocking
the soccer ball against the fence
I remember throwing a baseball
against the wall
only occasionally got angry
when it didn't ricochet
He must feel the same way
a couple skateboarders
fly by
How I remember
my hours of rapture
on a skateboard
before I had
problems problems problems
I hear voices
my knees are bad
I can't play golf
I do crosswords
I do math
problems problems problems
Sunday afternoon

montmartes

At home on the north wall is a print
by Utrillo
aunt Liz bequeathed it to me
a favorite possession

I'm trying to draw the figures
he uses for people
his people are fascinating

they're not stick figures but they're
not fully developed

they should be easy to copy but they aren't

I tried to make them with a palette knife
and I made some figures my own
certainly not fitting his Montmartes figures.

but maybe they'll do for my purposes
since I have no purpose but to make
a painting ------

repose

That's what art is about.
Not quietness, stillness,
nor separateness, harmony, radiance
so much.
Just repose.

pressure

The weatherman
puts up the map,
talks of pressure areas.
The map is
Washington/Oregon.
I am an Oregonian,
but today
I look on Washington.
You can almost feel
the slightly warm rain,
the apples, the cherries.
Is Washington a simpler smaller
kinder place than Oregon,
or does this Oregonian
feel some pressure today?

mooch

Dave bought his wife
the last bouquet
of red white and blue carnations.
It was the fourth of July,
and they made quite a sensation.
Fireworks,
red white and blue carnations.
I myself
read the Mutts comic,
and Mooch had his own flag,
a little pink flag.
It's the fourth of July.
There are no fireworks
here.
I read the Mutts comic.
Mooch
flies a little pink flag.

tri-met lift

my happiest hours
are spent on the lift bus
I do some city watching
and some deep thinking
I show the driver my pass
and take my seat
strap myself in
Ready for the ride
to Kaiser to Folk-Time
or Fred Meyer
If I were a kid
I'd say 'whee'
but I'm older
iller
(why I get to take the lift)
I could never drive a bus
but I can do something can't I
for now I'm disabled
and enjoy the ride
they provide
they: Candace Craig Randy
      June Terry Kathy
How they drive that bus
put down the lift
Some are conversational
I don't say much
I'm lost in thought
but I love my time
riding the lift bus.

terrible habit

I broke 2 habits. smoking, drinking.
thank god i quit smoking. drinking is
more problematic. I really think it
helps me at times. how you may ask.

to have a bit of nerve at times.
with wenches for example to loosen
my tongue with some people.
and then there is analyzing poems
or doing housework. a little beer helps.
courage of a kind. But I don't drink.
my meds say not to. and my mental illness
is too precarious to add alcohol
to the mix.

rhododendron

dying is easy for some
I'm an Oregon boy
I'm not used to dying!

oh I can go to a mental hospital
Do math
and paint and drink
like Utrillo

but it all comes down to
a gentle rain
a Rhododendron

Cornell Pink
Starbright Champagne
Starry Night
Pendulum
Northern Delight

it all comes down to
a gentle rain
a Rhododendron.

firenze

arrivederci Roma
vado a Firenze
con due amici

buono pomeriggio Firenze
andiamo il museo
dopo avere di caffe
art e bellisima donne
vita e dolce
cerano fiori dovunque
arrivederla Firenze.

snap

He threw the plate against the wall
and stopped and stared
at the shards.
Why did he do it?
He'd had two beers.
Was that why?
No, he just had
in his mind,
in his imagination
that this is what you
do in your kitchen
if you stumble across
a plate.
Nondescript,
not an antique surely,
yes, you snap 'em.

He could almost
hear a voice say that
yes snap 'em,
and he remembered
his aunt Liz.
Family rumor
had it
that
she threw plates
at her brother Bill
when they lived
together,
that
she was
a little

unhinged.
Maybe she
did snap plates
at uncle Bill.
Was she a pro?
Could I have
learned from her
her technique?

The voice
kept saying
you snap 'em.
I hadn't broke
anything.

but was
the godfather
sneaking up on me
I had a set
of china
would I smash the
whole set like
the girl in the movie

well it was
just a movie
and I did
like my set
of china
oddly enuf
it had been
aunt Liz's.

fly

a fly came by
hurrying on his way
i didn't think to swat him

he looked like a preacher, a parson
all bundled up
hurrying by.

gargoyles

To be or not to be that is the question.
But the question becomes, is Hamlet mad,
and the question becomes, am I also?
On the surface the answer seems simple.
Hamlet is mad as I am,
after all he talks to a ghost,
he sees a ghost.
Similarly I hear voices.
We're both nutcases.
But one ponders the question
how did Hamlet become mad
and how did I.
Hamlet has our sympathy.
His father has been murdered by his uncle.
His mother has proved weak,
then his girlfriend commits suicide.
Who wouldn't go mad?
We understand he's under a lot of pressure.
Some feel sympathy for him. Others don't
Yes, Hamlet has our sympathy.
Do I
becomes the question.

river

I'm out on the Clackamas
with my trout pole and net
and my boots
which often are tennis shoes
it's very lonely
a jay comes swooping by
a few crows look standoffish
I feel I'm going insane
the water
the blueness
the greeness
the yellow sun
All of a sudden
I resign myself
I'm not crazy!
I'm out on the river!

forget-me-not

there's a small field
of forget-me-nots
on my walk

and a solitary black tulip
that I call 'my death'
Sue says its purple tho
it only looks black

if I hang myself
I'll get purple first
and then be black

a noose
in my bedroom
where my light was

the voices
they'll be back
I'm a psycho
a black tulip
my death.

peace be with you

yes
please
help

I'm tired of the violence on TV
in the paper

pax pax vobiscum
I say it in Latin

when I was in college
I was a hippy
but I never had a peace shirt
now I do
and wear it proudly----

funny
yes I was a hippy
but didn't do the hippy crafts
now at folk-time I do:

tie-dyeing
potting plants
beading
ceramics
jewelry
well what Did you do
when you were a hippy? someone asked

Well smoked dope
protested the war

tornado

tuscaloosa alabama
joplin missouri
tornadoes
make us shiver
quiver
and sigh

is an earthquake
forthcoming
I'm a Portland guy
will the volcano breach again
or my illness flare up
I'll hear voices
again
again
again.

GG

they put her on a psych ward
and took away the scissors
I fear depression
I worry that i'm a suicide
a voice says end up in
a mental institution
Help GG Help

sweetness dont worry about me
it's true that i hate
 god country and the human race.
im just all boogered up as you say.

the cellist

I listen
what do I want to hear
something gay or joyful
often I hear
something sad
and mournful

what is the cellist message:
that we should care
or not at all

but mainly mostly
I have found
the cellist wants not to be profound
but contemplative.

the road ahead

I try not to look back.
Yesterday it seems
I was a nervous wreck.
I'll go crazy if I think
what do I lack.
For today i will survive,
keep planning, keep trying,
take a new tack.
Mental illness
is difficult,
and yet
its a pretty world at times
even when it doesn't rhyme.
I have to believe
its a pretty world at times.

lipton tea

It's a good thing
Herms,
my hamster Hermes,
isn't a lady.
I see into his boudoir,
his kitchen
where he eats,
and I watch
him at his wheel,
and I watch him
preen himself,
drink water,
and eat carrots.

The big difference
between Herms
and me,
I guess, is
I drink tea.
Pot after pot
of Lipton's tea.

therapy

I'm writing these poems
I'm in therapy
for years
therapy
and deadly pallor
I hear voices
a voice says to jump
off a ledge, a bridge
out my window
Martha
I appeal to you
I'm in therapy
a voice says
to kill people
Martha
I appeal to you.

on the way to freedom

why do they hate him so much
the affordable health care act
Obamacare

why do they hate him so much
I don't
I like him
I love him

And
we're on our way to freedom.

ice

Suicidal on a Sunday night,
what else is new?
Yet this night I was
thirsty and went to the icebox
and noticed there was no ice
and this ritual of making ice
this simple science question
what is ice
made me forget my plans
for self-destruction.
No booze,
diet cola sufficed.

tulips

I'm a failure.
I can't write
about the tulips.
I want to write
a poem.
Sublime
wonderful
four yellow tulips
in a wine glass vase.
Why can't
I write a poem
about the four tulips?
Maybe to comprehend
a tulip
requires sorest need.
I'm a failure,
and now I can
write my poem.

finis

my toy pig

My toy pig
fell over,
and I let it
rest a couple days.
And then the day came round
to turn up the pig
that was upside down.
My toy pig
and I waited
with bated breath
for the moment
I put the pig
back on his feet,
for I pondered the notion
am I free.
I needn't
right the pig,
there's no law saying so
just gentle decorum
and some ways discreet
these were imponderables.
What do I do?
Right the pig,
is that what I should do?
And I guessed
it had as much
importance as
shutting a window
or straightening a chair.
Things with furniture
we dare.

Well you can guess how
the story ends.
I put the pig
my toy pig
so he stood up
and cursed the day
this all came up.

wave

the wave breaks
into little rills
over my feet gently
the water is cold
I'm wading in the ocean
a favorite pastime

the ocean sends
little rills
white covered
clear and cold
a little splash
I'm wading in the ocean

for a moment I'm a child
there are no little
screams of joy tho
I'm wading in the ocean.

rollie

the dog jumped up on my lap
his name is napoleon
he's a dachsund

on my walk we saw 2 bulldogs
deb says they're expensive.

rollie wasn't expensive
got him at the humane society
he was one of six energetic pups
the night i brought him home
he fell off my bed.
something he would do often.

I called him rolls
he loved life
stupid brute little animal
knew nothing of perfidy
yet could get in trouble
i looked for him often
when he got lost

rolls led a happy life.
i'll never see him again
but remember aye verily.

magic

I showed Amalia
the rubik's cube
and solved it
She waited with
large eyes
and yesterday
I showed her
some card tricks
But her eyes were
not quite as wide
Oh her tongue was blue
with kool-aid all right
she tried my trick
and i was the
one with wide eyes
Something had changed
I could see
or so it seemed
her children
their eyes
And I thought
it was just
a magic trick.

withered

I threw out
the bowl of flowers
the petals withered
the leaves closed up

i could have set
fire to it
it would have lit up

and i thought of H.
a troubled life she had
emotions too

and mom
the old withered thing herself
yes

i threw out
the bowl of flowers
and remembered two
who reminded me
of flowers too.

in the tea shop

I walk in
  greeted by
            sweet smells
            oranges and spice
  Constant Comment
            that's nice
move along
stately princely
            tea cups
            china
            and tea
  Tetley's British Blend
 then the health section
   Green tea
            for the nerves
            for the bod
I feel calm
my spirits lift
a visit to the
  Old Tea Shoppe.

she bawled and cried

I was telling Dave
every family
can have one faucet
and no more--
a faucet being
a crier
a weeper

I consider
myself a
bit of a faucet
but not compared
to the real pros
those who make
an art of it
we're all potential faucets
awaiting some disaster maybe
a cause a reason
to turn on the spigots.
the point is you can
spend your life crying
and many do
or you can buck up
and stumble thru.

robins

digging a worm
stretching it out
leg lifts
early morning
television
exercise shows
Robins
early bird
the worm
exercise
Robins.

in the shower

che gelida manina se la lasci riscaldar
cercar che giove al buoi non si trova

well i don't sing opera in the shower.
and I don't sing much. Mainly cuz Dagwood
does and i don't want to emulate him.
I already do enuf. I call a repair job
a Dagwood. meaning I do part
of the repair and then call the
repairman. a Dagwood.

writing group

It is good to be here.
Ken is sick. But gloria can take over.
It's good to be somewhere
I'd of thought I might be dead by now.
My health is that poor.
I'm often suicidal,
but I don't have the courage to do that.
I'm not bipolar,
but I do have highs and lows.
Life for example
seems like this beautiful mysterious thing,
but also dross ugly vague stupid.
Why am I here then?
To have fun for one thing.
Itry to surround myself
with beautiful things
and (ha ha ha!) beautiful people.
Failing that
I try to have fun.
Failing that
I write.
I am a writer.

six pack

I have
three six packs of pop,
stacked up in the kitchen.
I looked at them
and they turned into my little dog rollo.
It is not beer.
It offers no charm
cept refreshment.
And yet it turned
into my dog
the six packs of pop.

I'm doing magic these days,
usually card tricks.
I have yet to
make a dog appear,
a dead one especially.
Refreshment.

ice cream truck

i stumble out drunk
lift my finger
to the good humor man

how often have i written
about the ice cream truck

that insane crazy music
the birds chirruping not chirping

where is my gramps
to buy me ice cream

where is my gramme
to save me from
the tires of the truck

and mainly mostly
i give a --------.

scrabble

Dan is coming over
to play scrabble
Saturday
we'll have a
relaxed game
and maybe
I will suggest chess
and profer a game
we'd better play
a relaxed game
For
chess is
an unnerving
battle of the wits.

humane society

winter 2012

McPike (dog)
is a handsome 4 year old
McPike would do best
in a quiet calm home.

Tigger Roo
tabby cat
mild mannered
diabetic cat

Puff
a 6 month old bunny

Scooter
is a cat with 9 lives.

Joey Bell
11 month old terrier mix
a little nervous.

Human society:
Charley Norm Bob Mike Tom
all dead alas.

sexuality

another way of saying this is that
all our problems are sexual ones.
its easy for me to say since sex
has always been a problem.
For some lucky people it is not
a problem I guess.
I say I guess cuz the girl I knew
who had no sex problem had sex
problems indeed.
she had lovers. that seemed as strange
as having no lovers.

tribute

Mom's friend has alzheimer's
mom says she talks about dead people
all the time.
Mom is 94
she is forgetful too
she remembers Ireland tho
a farm, a ship, a new land
Now mom talks of nasturtiums
shovels, dirt
a lamp and a spade
I love you mom.

sculpture

At the beach
at the cove are sea gulls sea swans
flying flapping

two green as green trees
a few boulders
and waves
plenty of waves a calm day a slight breeze
the gulls hold sway
it is their day

I am overcome briefly
by religious ecstasy
and think of my friend who sculpts in stone
while I use these poor old tools
a pen, paper and a damaged brain.

death

for a bitter Mary Oliver

when it's sleepy time
down south

I took a bottle of pills
drank a bottle of booze
Faulkner wrote of a character
who loves death

yes
life I cannot abide
it is gross
poop, snot, piss, vomit
sex ugh
life yecch
Death yes.